The Side-Hustle Millionaire: 24 side hustles you can start and SCALE

By Ton Jacques II

Introduction

No matter your current situation- whether you're working a job to pay the bills or whether you own your own business- there's infinite space above you. Everybody at every level of success has the opportunity to build additional income streams and reach new heights. This is not something that's reserved for certain people. Anybody with any schedule can spend a few hours each week to build additional streams of income. Success is never final. We must always continue to grow. This book is here to get your creative juices flowing. It will share with you many different actual businesses you can start right now. Business does not have to be sexy to make money- it only has to provide value to others. Here are 24 side hustles you can start right now.

1) Start a Fence-Staining Business

Take a look at every single home in your neighborhood. What do they ALL have in common? That's right, fences. Every house has fences. Now, how many fences do you see that could use a little freshening up? More than likely, almost all of them unless they're brand new.

On average, homeowners pay between $1200-$4800 to have their fences stained. Factors that weight on pricing include fence size, interfering vegetation, number of coats to be applied, and paint/stain type. First, you'll want to do your research on the different types of brushes, paint sprayers, techniques, etc. YouTube is great for all of this.

Once you've figured out the process and cost factors, set a monthly goal. Let's use the low end for the sake of being conservative. Assume you're able to complete a stain job in 1-2 days. This means that if you just do 1 job per week on the weekends, you could earn an extra $4,800 per month. If you anticipate bigger projects that would rake in higher per-job rates, that number could be north of $10,000 per month. But how do we get people to let us stain their fences?

Start small and start local. You need people to know about your service. Use an app like Canva to create beautiful flyers that outline your offering. Make sure to include a free quote so that you can give people an idea of what the cost would be to do the job. Once you've ordered your flyers, it's time to put together a system for distributing them to homeowners.

The 2 main ways you'll likely opt to distribute flyers are A) door to door or B) via direct mail. Option A is going to be much more cost efficient but will require a little bit of your time. That's why deciding ahead of time which days of the week you're going to pass out flyers is key. When you go door to door, optimize your time by attempting to talk to every homeowner. In-person connection is a major factor when deciding whether or not to work with someone. If your competitor is just leaving their flyers on the door mat, one-up them and knock on the door to talk with the homeowner yourself! Small actions compound in big ways.

You'll want to have an online presence too in order to attract a larger customer base. Use local services like Facebook groups and Nextdoor to connect with homeowners in your neighborhood. Don't be salesy, instead share your offering and ask if they know anybody who could use a freshen-up on their fences. Be consistent and ask for business often.

2) Rent out pickup trucks on Turo

If you're not familiar, Turo is an app that allows you to rent out your cars to other people. People pay you a set fee per day that they use your car. As the owner of the car, you set your fee. Turo provides the insurance coverage so that both you and the renter are protected.

As an owner, you can make anywhere from $40-$300 per day, per vehicle. Factors that weigh on price include competition for the same vehicle type in your city, demand based on day of the week, and length of the trip. You can rent out any type of car on Turo, but for the sake of specificity and honing in on a niche- we're going to discuss pickup trucks.

So, why pickup trucks? For starters, most people do not own a pickup truck. Most people, when they have a need to move large items, need to rent a pickup truck of some sort. This goes for moving needs, trips to the dump, moving things to and from their office, the list goes on. Providing something required in a time of need as opposed to time of want is a sure way to grow a consistent stream of revenue. Let's look at some ways to acquire your first pickup truck to start your fleet.

First you'll want to do a thorough scan of the current available pickup truck inventory on Turo in your area. Take note of the daily trip rates being offered. Which truck models command the highest per-day rates? Which command the lowest? Which trucks have the highest number of trips? These are all factors that are absolutely critical in deciding which truck type to offer.

Once you've narrowed down which model you'd like to pursue, take to Craigslist to see what's available. You'll want to make sure the math checks out with the projected daily rental rate x projected days per month the vehicle is rented out. This will allow you to arrive at an acceptable purchase price. Keep in mind, you don't have to own the truck outright to rent it out on Turo. If you opt to finance the vehicle, just be sure your projected monthly revenue covers your monthly cost to service the loan.

Renting out your cars on Turo is almost an entirely passive way to make money. However, you do need to keep the cars clean and wash them between trips. Factor the cost to maintain the vehicles when coming up with projections. As you get the hang of the Turo business and start to build systems, you can grow your fleet and make 10's of thousands of dollars per month. The sky is the limit here.

3) Use AI to create logos for brands

Artificial Intelligence is on the fast track to serving us in our everyday lives. It's already moving at speeds beyond most people's level of understanding. Many savvy businesses and individuals are harnessing the power of AI to expand their output capabilities and create streamlined systems.

As with any new groundbreaking technology or infrastructure, those that are early to the party are generally paid handsomely. Many brands and individuals will shy away from AI in the early stages. Most mainstream adoption will come only after a wide general acceptance by the broader population becomes evident.

With this opportunity at hand, now is the time to become the AI expert in a field that almost all business have a need for- logo design. It's incredibly simple and just takes a few steps on your end. In fact, most AI tools are no more complicated to use than any other app or program.

Now, how can you build a business on the side with this?

Simple AI apps and programs like LogoAI.com will allow you provide businesses and individuals with logo design services. To do this, simply make an account on LogoAi.com. This AI powered tool works by using criteria that you provide it with to create thousands of incredible logo images. When you find one that looks good, you can Further customize it to your liking until you arrive at the perfect design.

Once you've made a couple of practice logos, create an account on Fiverr to advertise your Logo design service. When someone reaches out to hire you, ask them for their criteria and a brief description of what they want. Then, use this criteria to customize the logo for them in Logoai.com. You can offer them a set number of revisions included in their package. Be sure that the price you charge your customers allows for enough margin to turn a profit on each logo. Depending on download options , LogoAI will charge for some formats/options.

Another way to advertise your business is on LinkedIn. Connect with business owners and provide them with some samples of designs you've done for others. Aim to reach out to 10-20 business owners each day. Follow-up is key! If you don't hear back right away, try again. It takes consistency to earn business for the first time.

Create a simple landing page using Wix. Then, use targeted google ads to drive traffic that's searching for logo design to your landing page. When a business enters their information, reach out and ask them what kind of logo they're looking for. This is a great way to feel out the demand for the different keywords you use in your targeted ad campaign. When you find large traffic sources coming from a certain type of lead, double down on tracking down more leads like that.

So, how much can you make from offering logo design services to brands and individuals? Let's assume you charge $75-$130 per logo. If each logo costs you $40-$50 on LogoAI.com, that will leave you with a profit of $20-$85 per logo, which only takes you a few minutes to do! If only did 1 logo per day (about 5 minutes of your time) that's $600-$2500 per month you could earn. This is a powerful opportunity if played correctly. Get creative and scale this to a full time business! With proper attention to detail and persistence, you could scale to 10, 20, even 30 logos per day.

4) Become an Open-House Host

Successful Real Estate agents are often swamped on the weekends with a multitude of Open-Houses to tend to. It's common practice for realtors to reach out to outside parties to host their Open Houses for them for a fee. This allows them to be multiple places at once. The average Open House runs for 3-4 hours. Almost all Open Houses take place on a Saturday or Sunday. With nothing but your outgoing personality and some light store-bought appetizers to offer guests, you can host Open Houses for realtors any weekend you want!

How does this work? In many areas, you don't need to have a real estate license to host an Open House. You may find that there may be certain restrictions on what subject matter relating to the property you're allowed to discuss with guests as a non-licensed host- but it should not prohibit you from being able to host the open house and direct questions to the agent on the listing.

In order to start hosting Open Houses for real estate agents, you need to connect with a handful of them. There are many ways in which this can be done. As it turns out- real estate agents love talking to new people. You can easily find the contact information for most agents by using Zillow and clicking on the agent information attached to the listings in your area. Reach out via phone call, email, or text to a handful of agents each day and let them know you're a local open house host who would love to help out whenever they need it.

Another way to connect with many agents in your area at once is by visiting the local real estate brokerage's website. There, you'll find the agent directory. You can reach out to the entire office and offer each agent your hosting services. Let them know your rates and your accepted methods of payment. Also let them know you provide food/beverages for an extra fee if they'd like.

Don't forget about social media and LinkedIn! Reach out to your local real estate agents on their social media to connect on a more personal level. Let them know you'd be happy to host their open houses to free up some of their time. They will love this value-add proposition that you've offered.

So, how much can you make hosting Open Houses? You can charge $100-$150 per open house that you host. If you provide appetizers and beverages, you could charge $200+ per Open House. Another way to maximize earnings from being an Open House host is offering to put out signs for an additional fee as well. If you do 2 Open Houses each weekend you could earn an extra $1200 each month. Once you build relationships with more and more agents, you can even hire others under you to host open houses. This will allow you to scale and be multiple places at once, too.

5) Create your own Vintage-Clothing store on Etsy

Etsy is a website that allows small business and individuals to create their own online stores and sell directly to customers on the site. To set-up a store, it only takes a few quick steps. There's tons of opportunity with Etsy. We're going to discuss the vintage-clothing niche.

Selling vintage clothes on Etsy is a great way to grow a cash-flowing business. To start, head to your local Goodwill or second-hand thrift store. While you're at the store, have eBay pulled up on your phone. Shop the isles and when you find pieces of clothing that look intersting or stylish, look them up on eBay by searching for the information on the tag. You'll find listings for the same piece of clothing all over EBay.

How does this translate to turning a profit? Let's say you stumble across a cool old rock band's tour t-shirt that somebody didn't want. You search it up on eBay and find it's selling for around $40. The thrift store is selling it for only $5. Minus your shipping cost, that's a $35 profit! Every week or 2, head to the thrift store and restock your inventory. Keep lots of clothes on-hand so that you aren't constantly having to run to the thrift store!

In addition to selling on Etsy, you can also sell your vintage clothing finds on eBay. Price your items competitively to keep your inventory moving. The more research you put into discovering which items are best for selling on Etsy and eBay, the more you'll be able to earn. Once you start earning money from sales, you can boost your reach by running some paid ads. When you find something that works really well, always double down.

How much can you make selling vintage clothes online. There's no limit! E-commerce knows no limits. The more creative you get with hiring help, running larger ad campaigns, and scaling, the higher your income is going to be. Selling clothes on the side can earn you a couple hundred dollars a month with minimal effort. Or, you can earn 10's of thousands or even 100's of thousands and millions if you scale effectively and choose a niche to specialize in.

Specializing in a niche category of vintage apparel will help you stand out and will maximize your rate of success. If you're finding great traction with concert t-shirts, be the go-to concert t-shirt person. If it's vintage hats or memorabilia, specialize in one of those areas. Find ways to stand out and you'll reap the benefits.

6) Earn passive-income online from your recipes

By sharing your recipes online, you can generate huge sums of monthly passive income. To start, you'll need to create a simple blog page using a service like Wix. Once you've setup your blog page, you'll need a name. Something simple will do and make sure it's food/kitchen/baking related.

Next, you'll need to upload a few dozen recipes. The initial setup will take some time but will pay off in the long run if you stick to the plan. If you don't have a long list of favorite original recipes, try harnessing the power of AI to assist. Use programs like ChatGPT to help you put together a delicious catalog of recipes.

As you post your recipes on your blog. Write about them. Include the simple things like why you love the recipe, ideal occasions to serve it, and so on. Be mindful of the importance of SEO. Search Engine Optimization is a crucial part of earning money with your recipe blog. In order to earn money you will need to run ads. The more traffic you have, the more advertisers are going to pay you.

Let's look at some ways to drive traffic to your blog to maximize your advertising earnings

Start an Instagram and TikTok page for your recipes. Here, you'll shoot short clips of you making the recipes. Your face doesn't even need to be in the videos. Create an upload schedule so that posts are going out every day. Use relevant hashtags so that your post spreads to the right audience. It's very easy to build a following quickly on TikTok with good food content. In your videos or your captions, reference your recipe blog often. This will drive traffic from your social media pages to your website.

Once you start seeing some healthy monthly traffic, make an account with Google Adsense. This will allow you to embed Ad slots onto your recipe blog. Google will pair these slots with advertisers who will pay you for placement on your blog. The more traffic, the more money. With that in mind, your focus should be on creating fantastic content and building a fanbase on TikTok and Instagram.

When you're first starting off it may seem overwhelming to think about creating TikToks or Instagram reels. The reality is, it's something that doesn't need to take more than a few hours each week. Plan one single day per week to film 7 short recipe clips. Schedule the videos to post automatically throughout the week on social media. The more creativity you add to the process, the greater your chances of success.

So how much can you earn with your recipe blog? Well, Google Adsense pays $0.2-$2.50 for every 1,000 views. This is why it's wise to have as many recipe pages as you can on your blog. If you're generating 10k views per day for each recipe, that equates to about $20 per recipe per day. These numbers become staggering with scale. However, without driving the traffic, you won't see much of a return- so focus and become an expert at filming your recipe videos!

7) Start a car-detailing side hustle

Starting your own car-detailing business is one way to generate a ton of cash on the side. To start, put out flyers. Put them everywhere around town. Pass them out door to door in high-end neighborhoods, place them on bulletins around local businesses, pass them out at the gym, cast a wide net. Your flyers should have a QR code that take you to a landing page with a few different package options. Offer a low tier, lower priced option, a mid tier option, and full-service deluxe option.

It will take you 1-2 hours to do a full detail. You can charge $150-$300 per detail job. If you do just one or two cars each day, you can generate an extra $4,500-$9,000 per month in income.

Before you start, do a few practice details on friends cars and hone in on your different detailing offerings. You can get a complete car detailing kit on Amazon for under $30. Once you've gotten the hang of it, you're off to the races. Utilize tools like YouTube to learn the entire detailing process. When you provide excellent service to your customers, they'll hire you to come back week after week and month after month- giving you some fantastic recurring revenue.

8) Start a scalable Farmer's Market business

Farmer's Markets are gold-mines for small businesses. Anybody can apply to farmer's markets if they run a small business. Generally, farmer's market managers are looking for new vendors who have something unique to bring to the table. Additionally, they look to fill gaps where they're currently lacking. To start, go to your local farmer's markets and walk around and observe what kinds of vendors are selling there. What seems to be doing well? What seems to not be doing well? What is this market missing?

Once you decipher where there's a gap to fill. Start going to work on this niche. Let's use pastries for example. Let's say your local farmer's market is lacking a pastry vendor. You can learn a handful of 3-5 great pastry recipes and create a fun and catchy business name. Make sure the recipes are great so that others will be excited about them.

Once you get your menu down, you'll need to reach out to your city's health department to get a permit to sell homemade baked goods. Many counties offer these permits for just a couple hundred dollars. Also consult with a lawyer to figure out what other business docs you may need.

After you've taken the necessary steps with the city's health department, it's time to apply to the Farmer's Market. Many cities offer multiple markets per week. If yours doesn't, you can always apply to neighboring city's markets too. Share with the market manager all of the details about your offering and why it would be a success at their market. Once accepted, get an appropriate canopy tent and table to use for your booth. Take things a step further by creating a great banner for your booth, too.

During an average 5 hour market, food vendors can make hundreds or even thousands of dollars. With these earnings, scaling to other markets becomes very attractive. Once you find success at your first market which will take place only once per week, you can start applying to nearby markets to get a booth slot there too. You can be at multiple markets every week or even every day if you hire a few helpers to run your other booths.

Many folks earn full-time incomes with farmer's markets and the smartest vendors who scale widely make millions. This is a business that's not widely talked about and it's truly a hidden gem. Start as small as you want and grow as big as you want.

9) Import wholesale products from Alibaba.com and sell on Amazon with Amazon FBA

If unfamiliar, Alibaba.com sells consumer products in bulk at wholesale prices. When you buy products in bulk on Alibaba.com, you're paying just a small fraction of the retail price. Amazon FBA allows you to ship products to an Amazon warehouse, and then Amazon will handle all of the logistics and shipping whenever an Amazon customer buys that product. This allows you as an Amazon seller to leave all the heavy lifting to Amazon, and collect payments each month.

To find profitable products to ship off to Amazon's warehouse you'll need to download an Amazon research tool like AMZscout. This google chrome plugin shows you full breakdowns of every product on Amazon. You can see how many sellers are selling that specific product, how many units sell each month, what the Amazon FBA fees are for that product, and more.

The ideal products are those that are small and lightweight (So you can save on shipping costs when purchasing from Alibaba), those that sell thousands of units per month on Amazon, and those that only have a small handful or even 1 single seller that's selling that product on Amazon.

To start, create a seller's account on Amazon. This is a simple process but there are a few steps involved. Once you've got your seller's account all setup, it's time to narrow in on which product or products you're going to sell. It's important to do your research on AMZscout so that you find a quality product to start selling.

You've decided on your product. unless you've created your own brand around this product, you'll be selling on Amazon under the "generic"category. Before making a purchase of the product on Alibaba, be sure to thoroughly cross-compare with different sellers. You will find more favorable purchase terms the more you search around. When you've landed on the product that you'd like to move forward with- you can make your purchase.

It's a good idea to ship the products to your home first before sending them to Amazon so that you can inspect them and be sure everything looks good. Some Amazon sellers opt to ship the products directly to the Amazon warehouse, however, this can be risky if there are defects in the product you purchased.

Once you've inspected the products and everything looks good- it's time to send them off to Amazon. After this step, simply keep track of your inventory through the Amazon Seller Central portal. When inventory is running low, it's time to re-purchase the products from Alibaba,

As you first start as a seller with Amazon FBA, it's wise to do a small scale test-run in order to get a feel for the sell-through rate and so on. However, the ability to scale with FBA is as simple as placing larger orders with Alibaba. This is an opportunity that can start out as a side-hustle and scale into a 7-figure business. Finding an un-tapped niche is key.

10) Pressure-Washing trash bins

With a pressure washer and some cleaning solution, you can earn thousands of dollars per week by cleaning people's garbage bins. These are the large trash cans out on the street in front of people's homes. Almost all of these trash cans have never had a proper cleaning. When they get dirty from the constant flow of trash they start to produce very unpleasant odors.

This problem presents an incredible opportunity to provide value to homeowners with dirty trash cans. To start, create flyers using an app like Canva. You can create beautiful flyers and Canva will ship them right to your door. Once you get your flyers outlining your service offering, it's time to pass them out door to door in your neighborhood.

Next, you're going to need a pressure washer, some scrubbers, and cleaning solution. You can find all of this on Amazon for around $150. Before you do you first job for a customer, do a test run on your own trash cans or on a friend's trash cans to get the process nailed down.

In order to start getting customers, you'll need a consistent plan in place to spread the word and get your flyers out. Set 1 day each week where you go and drop flyers in the neighborhood. To best maximize your time, aim to do 100 houses each time you go out to drop flyers. This will also enable you to track how many jobs you're getting per 100 houses.

On average, most houses are going to have 3 trash cans. Let's assume it takes 15 minutes to clean each can, plus an extra 15 minutes for cleanup afterwards. This equates to roughly 1 hour per job. Since cleaning trash cans is a job that many homeowners prefer to outsource to people like you, you can charge $150-$300 for your service. With these rates, you can rake in an extra $1,000-$2,000 each week doing just 1 job per day. That's $4,000-$8,000 in extra income each month just by cleaning 1 homeowner's trash cans per day.

As you grow a larger customer base, you can offer recurring service every 2, 3, or 6 months. You can also hire helpers to clean cans for you for an hourly rate. This way you can scale your business into something much bigger.

11) Send in sports cards to PSA for grading

What does it mean to send in sports cards for grading? In the world of sports cards, trading cards, and memorabilia- the practice of "grading" refers to when you send in a sports card or trading card to a company called "PSA", and they send your card back with an official "grade" from 1-10. If you've ever seen a sports-card in a glass case, it's likely a graded card. Collectors are constantly on the hunt for cards that are graded 8, 9, or 10. The only trouble is, you won't know the grade of a card until you send it into PSA and they assign it a grade based off it's condition.

When PSA grades cards, they use high level examination software that carefully scans cards for imperfections, creases, dents, tears, and so on. Some of these imperfections are nearly impossible to see with the naked eye. However, a seasoned enthusiast can usually have a general idea of what a card's grading may be simply from experience. So, how can you turn this information into a business? Let's dive in.

To start, you're going to need to familiarize yourself with the eBay card market. Search up any player or Pokémon character's card you'd like on eBay and see what they're selling for.

The key is spotting the difference in price between the ungraded cards and the graded cards. Of course, you'll need to compare apples to apples here meaning you can't compare a Barry Bonds card with a Tom Brady card. Instead, you need to look at what an ungraded Barry Bonds card sells for versus what a graded 8, 9, or 10 Barry Bonds card sells for, for example.

When you find a card with a wide margin between the ungraded listings and the graded listings, you'll need to start looking at the quality of the ungraded cards and compare them with the quality of the highly rated graded cards. You do not want to purchase any cards that have any visible imperfections whatsoever. If you can see an imperfection from just the photos- it's likely going to recieve a very poor grade and therefore sell for a low sum of money, thus wasting your time. Instead- focus on the mint condition cards.

When you find a card you want to move forward with, check to make sure that the cost of PSA grading plus the shipping cost will allow you enough margin to turn a profit. The cost of PSA grading ranges from $15 per card all the way up to $600 per card for cards worth up to $10,000. (yes, cards trade for that much!) Always project a lower grade than you hope for. We all want our cards to come back from PSA with a big shiny "10", but the reality is there will be many 6's, 7's, and 8's.

When you act with patience and employ a conservative strategy, you don't need to flip many cards to make a great profit in this game. With consistent eyes on the market and when you know what you're looking for, deals become obvious to you. You can make $500-$1000 on a single card if it comes back a 10. For the cards that come back lower than say, a 7, you can create a separate collection and sell bulk packs on eBay, too. This will allow you to recoup some investment from the cards that end up not being big winners.

In order to run a profitable card flipping business on eBay, patience is number 1. If you act erratically with your purchases and buy cards with "hope" or just for the sake of buying them- you will not see the returns that you hope for. Instead, study the market and act with reason. This is a great way to make some great money right from your cell phone.

12) Create service-provider lists for neighborhoods

For every neighborhood, there are hundreds of local businesses that cater to the residents. What you're going to do is connect (in person) with local business and offer them a spot on your "Neighborhood Service Providers"list. This list is going to go out to all of the residents in a given neighborhood where these local businesses offer their services. A service provider list is simply a list of highly rated local businesses that people can refer to when they need work done on their house or when they need certain jobs done.

The purpose of the list is to provide value to local homeowners by giving them a handy go-to reference sheet of businesses to use when they're in need of a specific service. The vendors on this list will get tons of exposure by being in every household in the area that they serve. It's a win-win for both parties.

So where do you come into play and how can you earn an income from this? Simple. Since there's huge value for businesses to have such great exposure by making the list, you're going to charge them a flat fee for a spot. You can charge based on how many other similar businesses are in the area. For example, if there's only 1 plumber in the area, you'll likely charge him less than if there were 10 others to compete with.

On the flip side, if you approach a local plumber with your offering and there are 10 other plumbers in that same area, he's going to have to pay a little bit more given the fact that there's competition for plumbing business in this market. Your list can be as long as you want but the focus should be on quality candidates that will do a good job for the neighbors to which you provide the list. Be sure to dig into reviews before reaching out or going to meet with businesses.

Examples of business types that people are often looking for referrals for include plumbers, flooring companies, carpet cleaners, house cleaners, gardeners, roofing companies, pest care companies, tree care companies, fencing companies, contractors, handymen, auto mechanics, and any business that relates to the home.

You can charge whatever you want for a spot on the list. However-given the fact that you're essentially offering print advertising services- you'll want to keep your prices in-line with other print advertisers in the area. Common local print ads can run anywhere from $60 to $80 up to $120. This all depends on size and detail of the ad as well as how many eyes will be on it. That said- let's say you're charging $75 on average. For each neighborhood you do- your lists could contain 50-60 different businesses. That's potentially $4500 that you could earn for each service provider list you put together! Expand and scale by going to different neighborhoods and creating more lists. This is a great way to become a connections person in your city. Many opportunities can arise from being the go-to person for referrals.

13) Flip couches using OfferUp

If you're unfamiliar, OfferUp is an app that allows people to buy and sell items from one another locally. It's a marketplace similar to Craigslist. On both OfferUp and Craigslist, people give away couches and other furniture for free everyday. There are many reasons why people may give away a couch for free. Most of the time, it's because they're moving and they have nowhere else for the couch to go so they list it for free on these marketplaces as a last resort.

On the same marketplaces, you'll find couches in the same condition as the free listings, but listed for $200, $300, $400, or more. Since so many people opt to get a new couch whenever they move- there's huge opportunity lying within these free listings. If you have access to a pickup truck and an extra room or garage space to store a couple of couches- you could be in a position to make some of the easiest money of your life. It will only require a bit of heavy lifting.

To start- become familiar with the condition of a majority of the couches that are actually selling on OfferUp or Craigslist. Then, cross-reference with the free couches that are listed. When you find a free couch that appears to be in great condition, go check it out.

You can probably tell where this is going. When you find free couch in great condition. Take it home with you and take some great photos of it. Then, post it up on all local marketplaces that allow neighbors to buy and sell goods. Think Craigslist, Facebook Marketplace, OfferUp, Nextdoor, etc. Create outstanding listings and price the couch where you see appropriate.

When priced well, items like couches sell very quickly and often with lots of interest. If you have enough space to store multiple couches, you can start a small inventory. If you assume a profit of a few hundred dollars per couch- you can see that you can make some pretty good cash simply by flipping free couches. All it takes is a little elbow grease.

If you really optimize your systems, you can scale this into a much bigger business. Think about what it would be like to run a small warehouse where you're constantly flipping couches from various sources. Become a pro and constantly find ways to go bigger.

14) Sell baked goods through local cafes and restaurants.

You probably didn't know that there's a business behind providing cafes and restaurants with pre-made food products to sell to their customers. Whether you take advantage of your local "Cottage Food" laws or if you rent out an hourly commercial kitchen to prepare food- you as an individual can sell your baked or prepackaged food goods to cafes and restaurants. And the best part is- they will actually buy from you! That is- if your food product is unique and tastes great.

So what is a Cottage Food law? Cottage Food laws vary widely from state to state. In short- obtaining a Cottage Food permit from your city's health department allows you to sell food products made at home to restaurants, stores, cafes, and more, depending on where you live. This means that you can bake cookies in your home kitchen and then sell them to your local cafe owner to sell in their cafe.

The alternate route to selling food products to cafes and restaurants is by renting out a commercial kitchen space by the hour to prepare your food. Both routes work great for varying needs.

Once you decide on where you're going to legally prepare your food, it's time to decide what your product is going to be. Do you have a great cookie recipe that everyone loves? Do you enjoy making healthy meals and meal prepping? Do you love to make salad? Whatever it is, figure out a way to turn it into a servable product. Think packaging, labeling, and portion size.

Next, figure out what it costs you to produce a single serving of your product. Let's say you're going to make and sell cookies. If it costs you $0.86 to make a single cookie and then $1.15 to package it, will you be able to make a profit from selling a batch to the cafe? To get an idea, see what similar products are selling for. This will give you a good idea of what you can charge the cafe owners for your product while still allowing them room to make a profit with retail sales. In most cases they'll want a minimum 30% profit margin. Run your numbers and when you find a recipe that makes sense- it's time to create incredible stand-out packaging.

To do this, use an app like Canva. Canva allows users insane flexibility in creating fantastic digital imagery. You can use a food label product template on the app and customize it to your liking. Spend time on this and create something that will really "wow"people. By having a beautiful visually appealing product your chances of sales are much higher.

So you have your product, you know all of your numbers, and you've gotten all the necessary permits. It's time to present your products to local restaurants and cafes. To do this- create a beautiful introduction box. Fluff it up and make it look like an exciting gift. Deliver these in person with customized hand written or typed letters. When you arrive at the business you're going to pitch to, ask for the manager or the individual in charge of buying merchandise. If they're there- explain your product, offer them a sample, and let them know why this will be a success at their business. Share pricing details and methods in which you accept payment. Be prepared with all of your numbers.

If the person in charge is not there, simply leave it with an employee and make sure that you let them know who you need it to get to. Then, follow up by checking in every couple of days until you connect with the person in charge.

You can scale to millions of dollars in revenue by supplying restaurants with pre-packaged products. Cast your net wider and wider and expand your production capabilities by hiring a few helpers. The more locations you're able to get your products into- the more revenue you can generate. Start small and build repeatable systems. Nail down your numbers and then strategize how you can grow. You can take your product online, to grocers, and so on.

15) Offer monthly deep cleaning services to local gyms and hotels

When it comes to gym equipment and free-weights, it's rare that they undergo a proper deep cleaning. Every gym and hotel has a cleaning crew on staff. They're constantly cleaning the common areas, changing the trash, cleaning the bathrooms, and cleaning all of the high-traffic areas of the facility. When it comes to the individual dumbbells, weight plates, benches, and yoga mats- they almost never get properly disinfected and sanitized. These are actually some of the most used items in the building and are absolutely covered in germs and bacteria.

By focusing on this niche area of sanitization within gyms and hotel gyms, you can set yourself up to accrue revenue from various sources each month. Create a nice flyer using Canva and layout your offering. Decide on how long it will take you to sanitize a large gym and come up with your pricing accordingly. You can also offer free quotes on the flyer. Next- you're going to visit all of your local gyms and speak with the general manager. Bring some data on bacteria growth and share with them how their equipment is likely crawling with germs. Layout your service and kindly ask them for their business.

The more gyms and hotels that accept your offering to clean their weights each month, the more monthly revenue you'll bring in. With large gyms that take 1-2 days, you can charge upwards of $1,000 for these jobs. With only a few of those every month, you could earn as much as a full-time salary.

To scale, you could hire a couple of helpers to get jobs done in a fraction of the time. You could eventually dispatch entire crews to multiple locations each day. Always go bigger.

16) Create UGC (User-Generated Content)

UGC stands for User Generated Content. User generated content is content made by everyday individuals using or showcasing products or services. As part of the newest social media marketing wave, brands are paying individuals to create UGC with their products and/or services. You don't even need to have a large following to create UGC content. In most cases, as long as the brand can repost your content on their social channels, that's all that's required!

So, how do you get paid? There are a few ways to start earning money by creating UGC. The first is by setting up an account on Fiverr to promote your UGC services. Film a few examples of you enthusiastically using a product or service. You'll upload these on your Fiverr account so that brands can get a sense of your personality and video style. You can set your own rate however you'd like. A few ways to set rates could be by charging per :30 video, for example, or by charging for a bundle of videos.

In addition to Fiverr, TikTok is also a fantastic place to earn money from producing UGC. Tiktok has different monetization features that allow everyday creators to earn money by posting UGC content.

As you first start, visit the TikTok marketplace and find products that pay a commission when you drive a sale. You'll create videos using these products.Expiriment with different video styles and find what converts to sales the best. Without an expansive portfolio, you'll likely earn $5-$10 per post. However, as you build up a library of quality UGC for brands to refer to, you can earn thousands of dollars per post! The key with UGC is consistency and experimentation. This is still a very new concept that many brands have not taken full advantage of yet, so being on the forefront can potentially pay handsomely down the road with some dedication.

As with everything else, cast a wide net and be sure you're taking advantage of all of the programs and opportunities available to you. Another place to earn as a UGC creator is Upwork. Many small creators are bringing in 5 figures each month simply by being consistent and trying new things.

17) Generate QR codes on Fiverr and Upwork

This is perhaps the simplest side hustle in this guide. If you know how to copy and paste a URL, you're ready to start earning cash from generating QR codes. To start, create a seller's account on Fiverr and Upwork. Your offering is simple- you'll create QR codes for people's websites. Many people simply don't know how to generate a QR code that directs traffic to their website. However- generating a QR code is as simple as copying the website URL and pasting it into an online QR code generator. It requires zero technical know-how.

Generating a QR code takes under a minute to do from start to finish. This means that you can earn extra cash with virtually no time commitment. Set up your offering on Fiverr and Upwork to showcase some example QR codes you've created. Pricing will vary depending on how many other sellers have similar offerings. Price your service competitively and make your listing stand out from the rest. Generally- you can charge $5, $10, $15, even $20 for a single QR code.

To further promote your service- you can connect with businesses on social media, LinkedIn, and other platforms.

Ask them if they have any QR codes to direct customers to their site. If not- send them the link to your Fiverr or Upwork account and offer to create one for them. Mention that they can use this QR code on marketing pieces to easily drive customer traffic to their website.

Furthermore- offer your service to local restaurants. During the pandemic, many restaurants adopted QR codes for their menus and haven't looked back since. This allows them to save big on printing costs from printing new menus month in and month out. For those that are still using traditional menus- reach out and see if they'd like to try out a scannable QR code to place at each of their tables for customers to scan when they sit down.

Get creative. This does not take much time and is a great way to earn some extra money. Will you get rich off generating QR codes? No. But you can certainly pay off some bills by doing so!

18) Market window cleaning services to Realtors

This is something that almost nobody ever thinks about because it's so niche. However- anytime Real Estate Agents take on a new listing, they need to get it cleaned and have the windows washed before the professional photography can take place. This is where you come in. Anybody can clean windows, including you.

Using an app like Canva- create beautiful flyers promoting your window cleaning service. Bring them to all of the local Real Estate offices and ask the front desk person if you may leave one for each agent. By being readily available and answering the phone when they call- you'll quickly become their go-to resource when they get a new listing.

On average, homeowners pay $250 for a window cleaning. Most window cleaners charge $10-$15 per window. Cast a wide net and connect with as many Realtors as you can. With just 1 cleaning per week you could earn an extra $1,000 each month. With 1 cleaning per day you could earn an extra $7,500 per month! There's power in widespread exposure. This is a simple service that is essential in the business of selling homes- so get out there and start marketing!

19) Make $30-$50 an hour Walking Dogs

Love dogs? Have a couple extra hours each week to walk around the neighborhood? You may consider offering dog walking services in your neighborhood. With so many folks back to the office for work, there are lots of furry friends stuck bored at home all day. Many people who work 9-5 jobs simply don't have the time or the energy to give their dogs the proper walks that they deserve. At the same token, most people love their dogs more than they do people! They will do anything to make sure their pet is happy and cared-for.

Start by creating some beautiful flyers on Canva and delivering them door to door in your area. The offering is simple- a 1-hour walk in exchange for a flat fee or hourly rate. Most people will pay $30-$50 for a 1-hour dog walk with a trustworthy individual like yourself. Offer a complimentary introduction meeting where you can come by and meet the dog and the owner. When you make a connection- figure out what frequency will best suit this dog. In some cases- owners may want you to walk their dog everyday! Others may opt for once per week. Regardless- this is a system that will create a recurring revenue stream for you.

With a just handful of recurring clients, you can earn a hefty income each week. Assuming 2 walks each day at $50 a pop- that's an extra $3,000 per month in income. The best part? You get to enjoy yourself while you do it and get in your steps for the day too! As you start getting busier you can think about hiring help and paying an hourly rate while still earning a margin on each walk. Eventually you could even have a crew of dog walkers that you employ. Build the system and then strategize on scaling options. Larger scale (when done right) = larger earnings.

20) Start a Curb-Painting business

Ever notice the address numbers painted on the curb in front of every house? After a while they get so worn out and faded that you can't even read them. In many instances these address numbers will go years before being repainted. This causes problems for delivery people, emergency responders, and house guests when trying to locate a residence.

Luckily, all that's required to freshen these things up is some black and white spray-paint, some painter's tape, and a stencil. To start, practice on your own home or on the home of a friend or relative. This way you can get the hang of it before offering your service to the public. Next, go door to door and offer your service to homeowners. Explain to them the risk of not being found by delivery people and emergency responders in the event of an emergency. Also explain to them how it will freshen up the look of their home by having a crisp looking address.

For each address you repaint, you can charge $25-$50. Each one should only take around 20 minutes to complete. To make best use of your time, bring along some flyers with you to leave for the homeowners that aren't home when you knock.

With an optimized system in place, you can knock out 3 houses per hour- potentially earning over $100 per hour! Take before and after photos of some of your jobs to show prospective homeowners the difference.

As with everything, check with your local ordinances and make sure you are legally compliant.

21) Put on group workout classes at the neighborhood park

Got a knack for fitness? Turn your knowledge into money by offering daily or weekly exercise classes at your local park. Whatever your niche is, whether yoga, aerobics, dance, calisthenics, boxing or some other form of exercise- there's an audience of people who'd be thrilled to take part in a group workout class run by you.

To start, identify what kind of workouts you'll be leading. Let's say you have a background in boxing and that's what you're going to choose. First, you'll want to test out some different workouts that can be applied in a group setting. Utilize YouTube or TikTok for inspiration. Next, you'll need to make sure you have all of the necessary equipment for a full class. For boxing- this may be as simple as some jumpropes, some hand pads, and some yoga mats for abs. Don't overthink it.

Next, you'll need to attract locals to partake in your classes. Post flyers all around town advertising your classes. Go where the fitness-minded folks are. Think hiking trails, gyms, supplement shoppes and so on. In addition to posting flyers, you can also go door to door to advertise. Lastly- take your marketing efforts online on platforms like Nextdoor.

You'll want your classes to be full to give an energetic workout experience to attendees. Create a sense of urgency with your marketing by adding phrases like "almost full" or "only a few spots left". This will prompt interested people to sign up before the class fills up. As far as pricing goes, think $20-$40 per person as a starting point. With a class of 10- that's potentially $400 for an hour class!

Before starting- check to see which (if any) certifications are required to teach fitness classes. By building up a loyal client base- you could rake in thousands of dollars in revenue each month simply by leading others through a workout! To increase income- increase class sizes or frequencies.

22) Offer sign-service help to Real Estate Agents

Real Estate professionals have busy and hectic schedules. They often outsource tasks in order to make best use of their time. One task that many realtors Opt to outsource is putting out open-house signs on the weekends. In order to put out all of their signs before an open house, this would require them to leave their house or office up to an hour early. For many- that's simply time that they don't have. This is where you come in.

Creating a service around putting signs out for realtors is simple and just requires a bit of heavy lifting on your end. Having access to a pickup truck or SUV is ideal for this kind of service. However- you can certainly get it done using a sedan and taking a few extra trips. To start- send out a blast email to all of the local real estate agents in your area. You can find their contact info by visiting the directory on your local brokerage's website.

Additionally- you can create flyers to bring by real estate offices to leave for the agents. Your flyers should clearly outline your offering and state your availability and contact info. Let them know that you're a reliable resource to help them each weekend.

With a couple weeks of consistent marketing- you can build up a client base of 5-10 realtors that you help out each weekend. For a service like this you can charge $60-$100 per agent. Pricing will depend on how many signs they want you to put out and how spread out across town they want them. If you figure you help 4 agents every Saturday and 4 agents every Sunday- that's revenue of $3,200 per month you can generate all on your own with no help.

Now, if you hire help to serve more agents- these figures can grow. This is a great business to employ local high school kids to make some extra cash on the weekends. Eventually- you can hire help so that you don't even have to put any signs out yourself. Instead, you could act as the middleman between real estate agents and sign helpers.

23) Start a vending-machine business

Have you ever thought about what it would be like to own a vending machine and collect passive income each month? The good news is- this is a feasable business that anybody can start. Here's how it works:

In order to start a vending machine business you'll need two things: vending machines and locations to place those machines. In order to minimize your risk, you'll start out with securing a location to place your vending machine first. To do so, you'll need to offer a local business a cut of the monthly sales that your machine brings in. Another option is offering a flat monthly fee to have your vending machine inside of their business.

Start by calling local businesses with lobbies or waiting areas. Businesses like car washes, auto repair shops, and gyms make for great locations to run a vending machine out of. When you connect with the owner of the business, let them know that they can make a recurring income stream by allowing you to place your vending machine at their business. On top of that, it will also provide their customers with added value by offering snacks and beverages. It may take some work to lock in your first location- but stay persistent and keep your end-goal in mind.

After calling around to different businesses and visiting some in person to connect with business owners- you'll lock in your first location. The only problem is- you don't have a vending machine yet! No problem. Be sure to manage expectactions upfront and let them know that the install date will be up to 60 days out (to allow time to acquire a machine).

For your first machine- buying used is a great option. You can search on Craigslist or EBay for used vending machines. Here, you'll find great machines for $800-$2,000 depending on condition and brand. Make sure you test the machine before buying. Once you purchase your first machine- it's time to stock it with products. Buy in bulk to maximize your profits. Think Amazon or Costco for your inventory.

Setup a system for collecting payment with the business owner. Every month you can come by and restock the inventory and pay the business their share. Once you get your system in place that works well for you- you can think about scaling to more locations with more machines. There's enormous opportunity to scale vending businesses and while it's not completely passive- it's pretty darn close. You can make thousands of dollars each month with a well-optimized vending route. Always focus on growth and where you're going to expand to next.

24) Start an ATM business

Running an ATM business is very similar to running a vending machine business. First- you're going to need a location to place your ATM machine. Reach out to local gas stations, grocers, bowling alleys, and movie theaters. Ask them if they currently have an ATM inside of their business. If they answer no- they may be a perfect candidate. Offer them a monthly "rent" to host your ATM machine inside of their business. This is a win-win for them and for their customers.

Once you've connected with a business owner that agrees to let you install an ATM, it's time to acquire an ATM machine. You can get one on eBay for $1,800-$2,500. On average, you will be making $3 per transaction when people pull money out of your ATM. Be sure that you'll be able to make enough money from transactions each month to cover the rent that you'll be paying the business owner to have your machine there. It will take some studying of the daily traffic in order to come to reasonable projections of monthly revenue.

When you find success at one business, aim to double down on the same type of business for your next location. Keep doing what works. ATM routes offer great semi-passive income opportunities with some operators making 5-6 figures each month.

Closing

There are countless opportunities available to you right now to increase your income and grow financially. Running your own business is key in becoming financially independent. Be creative, be persistent, and always look at the longterm timeline. Don't get discouraged by short term rejection or failure; it's guaranteed. When you start seeing success from one of your ventures, put more energy into that. Continue to grow and scale and you can become wealthy beyond your wildest dreams.